Mastering Management

A Guide to Effective Leadership
Jules Beshears

Message From The Author

Iwas told , **"We are paid for our value and not our time."** As such, my books, on the surface, may seem somewhat lacking in terms of page count. What they lack in the sheer number of pages that tell stories about me growing up, or making my first million, etc., I choose to prioritize value. The books I write remove most of the fluff and are condensed, distilled, raw value that will hopefully change your life for the better.

This book is dedicated to my family, friends, and to all the entrepreneurs that chose never to give up.

Contents

1.

2.

3.

4.

5.

6.

7.

8.

9.

10.

11.

12.

13.

14.

15.

Chapter 1

The Art of Management: Essential Skills for Leaders

Introduction: In today's fast-paced business environment, the role of a manager is more critical than ever. Successful managers must possess various skills to lead their teams effectively, navigate workplace challenges, and achieve the desired results. This chapter will explore the essential skills required to become a successful manager and how to develop these skills to excel in your role.

1. Understanding Your Leadership Style: One of the first steps to becoming a better manager is understanding your leadership style. Your leadership style defines how you interact with your team, delegate tasks, and approach decision-making. By understanding your leadership style, you can tailor your approach to best suit your team and the organization's needs.

2. Building Trust with Your Team: A critical aspect of effective management is building trust with your team. Trust is essential for creating a positive work environment, fostering collaboration, and improving team performance. Managers can build trust by being transparent, consistent, and treating all team members fairly.

3. Communicating Effectively with Your Team: Clear and effective communication is essential for success as a manager. A manager must be able to express their vision and goals to the team and listen to their ideas and concerns. Effective

communication includes using the right medium for the message, such as face-to-face communication, email, or video conferencing.

4. Motivating and Inspiring Your Team: As a manager, you are responsible for motivating and inspiring your team. This can be achieved by setting clear goals, recognizing and rewarding good performance, and providing opportunities for personal and professional growth.

5. Delegating Responsibilities Efficiently: An effective manager must delegate responsibilities efficiently and effectively. You can build your team's skills, increase productivity, and reduce stress levels by delegating tasks. However, delegating the right task to the right person and providing the necessary support and resources is essential.

6. Developing Your Team Members: An essential aspect of management is developing your team members. You can build a high-performance team and create a positive work environment by providing opportunities for professional growth, training, coaching, and promoting continuous learning.

7. Managing Conflict Resolution: Conflict is an inevitable part of any workplace, and it's the manager's responsibility to address and resolve conflicts effectively. A manager must be able to recognize the root cause of the conflict, identify potential solutions, and facilitate a resolution that benefits all parties involved.

8. Time Management and Prioritization: Managing time effectively is crucial for a manager's success. By setting

priorities, creating a schedule, and avoiding time-wasters, managers can increase their productivity and achieve their goals. It's also important to delegate tasks effectively and delegate responsibilities to your team to reduce your workload.

9. Setting and Achieving Goals: As a manager, it's essential to set clear and measurable goals for yourself and your team. Goals provide direction, motivation, and a sense of accomplishment. By setting achievable goals and regularly monitoring progress, managers can ensure their team is on track to success.

10. Performance Management and Feedback: Performance management is an ongoing process that includes setting expectations, providing feedback, and addressing performance issues. Regular, constructive feedback can help team members improve their performance and increase their satisfaction with their work. Managers must also handle performance issues promptly and fairly to maintain a positive work environment.

11. Building a Positive Work Culture: An organization's work culture significantly impacts employee satisfaction and performance. Managers can build a positive work culture by promoting collaboration, recognizing achievements, and creating a supportive work environment. A positive work culture can increase employee engagement and motivation, leading to improved performance and a more productive team.

12. Navigating Change and Adaptability: Change is a constant in the business world, and a manager must navigate change effectively. Managers must be flexible, open to new ideas, and

adapt to new situations. By embracing change and being adaptable, managers can lead their teams through periods of change and help the organization remain competitive.

13. Managing Remote Teams: The COVID-19 pandemic has accelerated the remote work trend, and managers must now be able to manage remote teams effectively. This requires clear communication, setting expectations, and providing resources and support to ensure remote team members are productive and engaged.

14. Staying Current with Industry Trends and Best Practices: A successful manager must remain current with industry trends and best practices. By attending conferences, reading industry publications, and participating in professional development opportunities, managers can stay up-to-date on the latest techniques and strategies for effective management.

The art of management requires a combination of skills, including understanding your leadership style, building trust with your team, communicating effectively, motivating and inspiring your team, delegating responsibilities efficiently, and developing your team members. By developing these skills, you can become a successful and effective manager and lead your team to success.

Chapter 2

Understanding Your Leadership Style

Leadership is a complex and multi-faceted concept that encompasses many skills and qualities. To be an effective leader, it's crucial to have a deep understanding of your leadership style, as well as the styles of others. This chapter will explore the various leadership styles and help you determine your leadership style.

1. Introduction to Leadership Styles: Leadership styles are the different approaches that leaders use to influence, motivate, and guide their followers. The most common leadership styles include autocratic, democratic, laissez-faire, transformational, and transactional.

2. Autocratic Leadership: Autocratic leaders are those who make decisions without consulting others. They tend to have a dictatorial style and use their authority to control their followers. This style is often used when quick decisions are necessary and there's limited time for discussion.

3. Democratic Leadership: Democratic leaders involve their followers in the decision-making process. They listen to the opinions and ideas of others and encourage open and honest communication. This style is often used in situations where collaboration and teamwork are required.

4. Laissez-Faire Leadership: Laissez-faire leaders take a hands-off approach, providing minimal direction and allowing their followers to take the lead. This style is often used when the

leader trusts their team and wants to empower them to make their own decisions.

5. Transformational Leadership: Transformational leaders inspire and motivate their followers through their vision and enthusiasm. They focus on the development and growth of their team and create a positive and energetic work environment.

6. Transactional Leadership: Transactional leaders focus on exchanging rewards and punishments to manage their followers. They set clear expectations and provide incentives for meeting those expectations and consequences for not meeting them.

7. Understanding Your Leadership Style: You can complete a self-assessment questionnaire or work with a mentor or coach to understand your leadership style. It's important, to be honest with yourself and not just choose the style you think is the "best." By understanding your leadership style, you can identify your strengths and areas for improvement and make adjustments as necessary.

8. Flexibility and Adaptability: It's important to remember that no leadership style is perfect, and the best leaders can often adapt their style to the situation. By being flexible and adapting your style as necessary, you can be an effective leader in various situations.

Chapter 3

Building Trust with Your Team

Building Trust with your team is essential for creating a positive and productive work environment. Trust is the foundation of a strong working relationship and is vital for effective leadership. In this chapter, we will explore the various aspects of building trust with your team and provide tips for developing trust-based relationships.

1. What is Trust: Trust is the belief in the reliability, ability, or strength of someone or something. Trust is the foundation of all relationships and is essential for effective leadership.

2. Importance of Trust in the Workplace: Building Trust with your team is essential for creating a positive and productive work environment. Trust allows for open communication, helps to foster teamwork and collaboration, and enables leaders to achieve their goals more effectively.

3. Building Trust with Your Team: Building trust with your team requires effort and dedication from the leader. Leaders can build trust by being transparent, honest, and consistent in their actions and decisions. They can also build trust by showing respect, empathy, and compassion toward their team members.

4. Effective Communication: Effective communication is a crucial component of building trust. Leaders who are skilled communicators are better equipped to build relationships, resolve conflicts, and achieve their goals. Good

communication skills help leaders to create a positive and supportive work environment and foster teamwork and collaboration.

5. Consistency and Reliability: Leaders who are consistent and reliable in their actions and decisions are more likely to build trust with their team. When leaders are dependable and trustworthy, team members are more likely to have confidence in their leader and their ability to achieve their goals.

6. Providing Opportunities for Growth and Development: Leaders who provide opportunities for growth and development for their team members are more likely to build trust with their team. Providing opportunities for training, mentorship, and professional development shows that leaders value their team members and are invested in their success.

7. Resolving Conflicts: Leaders skilled at resolving conflicts are better equipped to build trust with their teams. Resolving conflicts fairly and equitably shows that the leader is committed to the well-being of their team and is working to create a positive work environment.

Building Trust with your team is essential for effective leadership. Leaders who can develop trust-based relationships with their teams are better equipped to create a positive and productive work environment, resolve conflicts, and achieve their goals. By building trust with your team, you can become a more effective leader and help your team reach its full potential.

Chapter 4

Communication Skills for Effective Leadership

Effective communication is a crucial component of effective leadership. Leaders who are skilled communicators are better equipped to influence, motivate, and guide their followers. This chapter will explore the various aspects of effective communication and provide tips for improving your communication skills.

1. The Importance of Communication in Leadership: Effective communicators are better equipped to build relationships, motivate their teams, and achieve their goals. Good communication skills help leaders to create a positive and supportive work environment and foster teamwork and collaboration.

2. Active Listening: Active listening is a critical component of effective communication. Leaders who are good listeners are more likely to understand the needs and concerns of their followers, and they're better equipped to respond to those needs in a way that motivates and inspires.

3. Verbal Communication: Verbal communication is another critical aspect of effective communication. Leaders who are skilled communicators can articulate their ideas and vision clearly and concisely, and they're able to communicate in a way that engages their audience.

4. Nonverbal Communication: Nonverbal communication refers to how you communicate through your body language, facial

expressions, and tone of voice. Leaders aware of the power of nonverbal communication can use it to their advantage to build rapport and convey their message effectively.

5. Written Communication: Written communication is another important aspect of effective communication. Leaders who are skilled writers can communicate their ideas and vision through reports, emails, and other written materials.

6. Effective Presentation Skills: Leaders who are skilled presenters are able to deliver compelling and engaging presentations. Good presentation skills help leaders to convey their ideas and vision in a way that inspires and motivates their audience.

7. Improving Your Communication Skills: There are several ways to improve your communication skills, including taking courses, working with a mentor or coach, and seeking feedback from others. It's essential to continually work on your communication skills and to be open to feedback and improvement.

In conclusion, effective communication is an essential component of effective leadership. Leaders who are skilled communicators are better equipped to build relationships, motivate their teams, and achieve their goals. By developing your communication skills, you can become a more effective leader and help your team reach its full potential.

Chapter 5

Motivating and Inspiring Your Team

Motivating and inspiring your team is an integral part of effective leadership. A motivated and inspired team is more productive, more engaged, and more likely to achieve its goals. In this chapter, we will explore the various aspects of motivation and inspiration and provide tips for leading a motivated and inspired team.

1. Understanding Motivation: Motivation is the driving force behind a person's behavior and actions. Understanding what motivates your team members is essential for effectively leading and managing them.

2. Theories of Motivation: There are various theories of motivation, including Maslow's hierarchy of needs, Herzberg's two-factor theory, and the Self-Determination Theory. These theories help to explain the various factors that influence motivation, including physiological needs, safety, belonging, esteem, and self-actualization.

3. Motivating Your Team: Leaders can motivate their team by providing recognition and rewards, setting challenging goals, and providing opportunities for growth and development. Leaders can also create a positive and supportive work environment, foster teamwork and collaboration, and provide opportunities for employees to have a voice and contribute to the organization's goals.

4. Understanding Inspiration: Inspiration is the spark that ignites creativity and motivation. Inspiration is often a result of a leader's vision and the sense of purpose they provide for their team.

5. Inspiring Your Team: Leaders can inspire their team by providing a clear and compelling vision, leading by example, and encouraging team members to pursue their passions and interests. Leaders can also foster creativity and innovation, provide opportunities for team members to develop their skills and abilities, and support their team members in achieving their goals.

6. Providing Recognition and Rewards: Providing recognition and rewards is an effective way to motivate and inspire your team. Recognizing team members' achievements and contributions helps build their confidence, increase motivation, and foster a sense of belonging.

7. Encouraging Teamwork and Collaboration: Encouraging teamwork and collaboration helps to build a positive and supportive work environment, foster trust and cooperation, and increase motivation and inspiration. Leaders can encourage teamwork by creating opportunities for team members to work together, promoting open communication, and recognizing the achievements and contributions of their team.

8. Empowering Team Members: Empowering team members is an effective way to motivate and inspire them. Empowerment involves giving team members the autonomy and resources

needed to achieve their goals while providing support and guidance.

9. Fostering a Growth Mindset: Fostering a growth mindset is essential to motivating and inspiring your team. A growth mindset is a belief in one's ability to learn, grow, and develop over time. Leaders can foster a growth mindset by encouraging their team members to embrace challenges, embrace failure, and pursue growth opportunities.

10. Encouraging Personal and Professional Development: Encouraging personal and professional development is crucial to motivating and inspiring your team. Providing opportunities for employees to learn new skills, pursue new interests, and advance in their careers helps to increase their motivation, build their confidence, and foster a sense of fulfillment.

11. Leading by Example: Leading by example is integral to inspiring and motivating your team. When leaders model the behavior and attitudes they expect from their team, they help create a positive and supportive work environment, increase trust, and build credibility.

12. Building Strong Relationships: Building solid relationships with team members is essential in motivating and inspiring them. When leaders take the time to get to know their team members, listen to their needs and concerns, and show genuine interest in their well-being, they foster a sense of connection and trust, increase motivation, and build stronger relationships.

13. Communicating Effectively: Effective communication is essential for motivating and inspiring your team. Leaders who communicate clearly, regularly, and respectfully help to build trust, increase understanding, and foster a positive and productive work environment.

14. Balancing Support and Challenge: Balancing support and challenge is important for motivating and inspiring your team. Providing the proper support and challenge helps foster a sense of purpose, build confidence, and increase motivation. Leaders who can balance support and challenge are more likely to help their team members achieve their goals and reach their full potential.

Motivating and inspiring your team is a crucial part of effective leadership. By understanding the various aspects of motivation and inspiration and applying the principles and techniques discussed in this chapter, you can become a more effective leader and help your team achieve its goals. Remember that leading a motivated and inspired team is a continuous process, and it requires ongoing effort, attention, and commitment.

Chapter 6

Delegating Responsibilities Efficiently

Introduction: Delegating responsibilities is an important part of being an effective manager. Delegating allows managers to focus on their most essential tasks while freeing up time and resources to help their team members grow and develop.

1. Understanding Your Team's Skills and Abilities: To delegate responsibilities effectively, it's important to understand the skills and abilities of each team member. By understanding what each team member is capable of, you can delegate tasks that are both challenging and achievable and help your team members to grow and develop.

2. Identifying Areas for Delegation: Identifying areas for delegation is an important part of the delegation process. To delegate effectively, you must identify tasks that can be delegated, assess your team's skills and abilities, and match tasks to team members based on their strengths and interests.

3. Setting Clear Expectations: When delegating responsibilities, it's essential to set clear expectations. This includes outlining the purpose and objectives of the task, establishing deadlines, and defining the desired outcome. Setting clear expectations helps to ensure that the delegation process is successful and that the delegated task is completed to the expected standard.

4. Providing Support and Guidance: When delegating responsibilities, it's important to provide support and guidance

to help team members succeed. This includes giving clear instructions, offering feedback, and being available to answer questions and provide support as needed. Providing support and guidance helps to build team member confidence and increase the likelihood of success.

5. Empowering Team Members: Empowering team members is an essential part of the delegation process. By empowering team members to make decisions and take ownership of their work, you can build trust, increase motivation, and help your team members to develop their skills and abilities.

6. Monitoring Progress: Monitoring progress is an integral part of the delegation process. By regularly checking in on the status of delegated tasks, you can identify areas for improvement, provide feedback, and help to ensure that the delegation process is successful.

7. Offering Recognition and Reward: Offering recognition and reward is an important part of the delegation process. Recognizing and rewarding team members for their hard work and achievements can increase motivation, build trust, and foster a positive and supportive work environment.

8. Balancing Delegation and Control: One of the challenges of delegation is finding the right balance between delegating responsibilities and retaining control over the outcome. It's crucial to delegate enough to empower your team members and maintain enough control to ensure that the task is completed to the desired standard. One way to balance delegation and control is to initially delegate smaller, less

critical tasks and gradually increase the level of delegation as you build trust with your team members.

9. Delegating to Multiple Team Members: When delegating responsibilities to multiple team members, it's essential to communicate clearly with each team member and ensure no overlap or confusion. You may also need to coordinate with other managers or stakeholders to ensure that the delegation process is seamless and that everyone is on the same page.

10. Delegating Remotely: In today's work environment, more and more managers are delegating responsibilities to remote team members. When delegating to remote team members, it's crucial to establish clear communication channels, set clear expectations, and provide regular check-ins and feedback to ensure that the delegation process is successful.

11. The Benefits of Effective Delegation: Effective delegation can bring many benefits, including increased efficiency, improved productivity, and increased employee satisfaction and motivation. Delegation also allows managers to focus on their most important tasks and provides opportunities for team members to grow and develop their skills.

12. Conclusion: Delegating responsibilities efficiently is an integral part of being an effective manager. By understanding the skills and abilities of your team members, setting clear expectations, providing support and guidance, empowering team members, monitoring progress, offering recognition and reward, and balancing delegation and control, you can delegate responsibilities effectively and help your team to succeed.

Chapter 7

Developing Your Team Members

Introduction: As a manager, one of your key responsibilities is to develop and support your team members so that they can achieve their full potential. By investing in your team members, you can build a more skilled, motivated, and engaged workforce that will help your organization to succeed.

1. Assessing Team Member Development Needs: To develop your team members effectively, it's essential to understand their individual strengths, weaknesses, interests, and development needs. This can be achieved through regular performance reviews, feedback sessions, and skill assessments.

2. Providing Opportunities for Growth and Development: One of the most effective ways to develop your team members is to provide them with opportunities for growth and development. This can include training and development programs, mentorship programs, and opportunities to take on new and challenging projects.

3. Encouraging Professional Development: Encouraging your team members to engage in professional development activities, such as attending conferences, workshops, and online courses, can help them to build their skills and knowledge and stay up-to-date with the latest industry trends.

4. Supporting Career Development: Helping your team members achieve their career goals and aspirations is an integral part of developing them. This can include providing opportunities for advancement, offering career coaching and mentorship, and supporting their pursuit of professional certifications.

5. Encouraging Continuous Learning: Encouraging a culture of continuous learning can help your team members to develop their skills and knowledge and keep pace with the changing demands of their role and the organization. This can be achieved by providing regular training and development opportunities, promoting self-directed learning, and recognizing and rewarding continuous learning efforts.

6. Providing Feedback and Recognition: Providing regular, constructive feedback to your team members can help them to identify areas for improvement and understand how they are contributing to the organization's success. Additionally, recognizing and rewarding your team members for their efforts can motivate and engage them and build a positive team culture.

7. Fostering a Positive Team Culture: Fostering a positive team culture that values learning, growth, and development can create a supportive and engaging environment for your team members. This can be achieved by promoting open communication, encouraging collaboration, and recognizing and rewarding team success.

8. Conclusion: Developing your team members is critical to being an effective manager. By assessing their development

needs, providing opportunities for growth and development, encouraging professional development, supporting career development, fostering a positive team culture, and providing feedback and recognition, you can help your team members to achieve their full potential and contribute to the success of your organization.

9. Case Studies: To help illustrate the concepts discussed in this chapter, consider the following case studies:

Case Study 1: Jane, a manager at a tech company, assessed the development needs of her team members and found that many of them needed to gain basic project management skills. She arranged for her team to attend a workshop on project management and provided opportunities for them to put their newly acquired skills into practice on real projects. As a result, her team was able to complete projects more efficiently and effectively, leading to increased productivity and customer satisfaction.

Case Study 2: John, a manager at a retail company, encouraged his team members to pursue professional development opportunities, such as attending industry conferences and workshops. He also offered to provide financial support for these activities and gave his team members time off to attend. As a result, his team members became more knowledgeable and confident in their roles, and they were able to bring new ideas and best practices back to the company, leading to improved business performance.

Case Study 3: Sarah, a manager at a marketing firm, fostered a positive team culture by promoting open communication, encouraging collaboration, and recognizing and rewarding team success. She also provided regular training and development opportunities for her team members and encouraged them to take on new and challenging projects. As a result, her team became more motivated, engaged, and productive, leading to improved team morale and better business results.

1. Key Takeaways:

- Assessing your team members' development needs is the first step in developing them effectively.
- Providing opportunities for growth and development, such as training and development programs, mentorship, and new and challenging projects, can help your team members build their skills and knowledge.
- Encouraging professional development, such as attending conferences and workshops, can help your team members stay up-to-date with the latest industry trends.
- Supporting career development, such as offering career coaching and mentorship, can help your team members achieve their career goals.
- Encouraging a culture of continuous learning, such as providing regular training and development opportunities and promoting self-directed learning, can help your team members develop their skills and knowledge and keep pace with changing demands.
- Providing regular, constructive feedback and recognition can help your team members understand their strengths and weaknesses and feel motivated and engaged.

- Fostering a positive team culture that values learning, growth, and development can help create a supportive and engaging environment for your team members.

1. Action Plan: To put the concepts discussed in this chapter into practice, consider the following action plan:
2. Assess the development needs of your team members by conducting regular performance reviews and feedback sessions.
3. Provide opportunities for growth and development, such as training and development programs, mentorship programs, and new and challenging projects.
4. Encourage professional development by offering financial support for attending conferences and workshops and offering time off to attend.
5. Support career development by offering career coaching and mentorship and supporting the pursuit of professional certifications.
6. Encourage continuous learning by providing regular training and development opportunities, promoting self-directed learning, and recognizing and rewarding continuous learning efforts.
7. Provide regular, constructive feedback and recognition to help your team members understand their strengths and weaknesses and feel motivated and engaged.
8. Foster a positive team culture by promoting open communication, encouraging collaboration, and recognizing and rewarding team success.

Chapter 8

Managing Conflict Resolution

1. Introduction: Conflict is an inevitable part of any organizational setting, and effective conflict resolution is a critical leadership skill. The ability to manage conflicts effectively can help to improve team morale, increase productivity, and enhance team relationships. In this chapter, we will discuss strategies for effectively resolving conflicts in the workplace.

1. Understanding Conflict: Conflict arises when people have differing needs, goals, values, opinions, or perspectives. It can arise from issues related to work tasks, resources, communication, or personal relationships. Effective conflict resolution requires a deep understanding of the root causes of the conflict and the needs and perspectives of the individuals involved.

2. Common Causes of Conflict: Common causes of conflict in the workplace include:

- Communication breakdowns
- Personality differences
- Competition for resources
- Different goals and priorities
- Perceptions of unequal treatment or recognition

4. Approaches to Conflict Resolution: There are several approaches to conflict resolution, including:

- Compromise: This approach involves finding a solution that meets the needs of both parties and involves some degree of concession by each party.
- Collaboration: This approach involves working together to find a solution that benefits all parties involved. This approach often requires open communication, active listening, and creative problem-solving.
- Competing: This approach involves a win-lose scenario, where one party gains at the expense of the other party. This approach is typically not recommended for resolving conflicts in the workplace.
- Accommodating: This approach involves giving in to the demands of one party in order to maintain good relationships. This approach can be effective in some situations, but it is important to consider the long-term impact on the relationship and the organization.
- Avoiding: This approach involves avoiding the conflict by ignoring it or delaying it. This approach is not recommended, as conflicts tend to escalate over time.

5. Steps to Effective Conflict Resolution: The following steps can help to resolve conflicts effectively:

- Step 1: Identify the conflict: Identify the specific issue or concern that is causing the conflict and the individuals involved.
- Step 2: Gather information: Gather as much information as possible about the conflict and the perspectives of the individuals involved.

- Step 3: Assess the situation: Assess the causes of the conflict and the needs and perspectives of the individuals involved.
- Step 4: Develop a plan: Develop a plan for resolving the conflict that addresses the needs and perspectives of all parties involved.
- Step 5: Implement the plan: Implement the plan for resolving the conflict and monitor the results.
- Step 6: Evaluate the outcome: Evaluate the outcome of the conflict resolution process and identify any areas for improvement.

6. Communication Skills: Effective communication skills are essential for conflict resolution. Good communication skills can help to build trust, foster understanding, and promote cooperation between the individuals involved in the conflict. Effective communication skills include:

- Active listening: Listen to the needs and perspectives of others and acknowledge their feelings.
- Open communication: Encourage open and honest communication between all parties involved.
- Empathy: Show understanding and concern for the feelings and perspectives of others.
- Clarity: Ensure that communication is clear and concise, avoiding ambiguity and misunderstandings.

7. Key Takeaways:

- Conflict is an inevitable part of organizational life, and effective conflict resolution is a critical leadership skill.

- Understanding the root causes of conflict and the needs and perspectives of the individuals involved is essential for effective conflict resolution.
- Different approaches to conflict resolution are appropriate for different situations, and it is important to choose the right approach.

Chapter 9

Time Management and Prioritization

Introduction: Time management and prioritization are critical skills for any manager. Effective time management and prioritization can increase productivity, reduce stress, and enhance overall job satisfaction. In this chapter, we will discuss strategies for effectively managing time and prioritizing tasks.

1. Understanding the Importance of Time Management: Time management involves effectively using your time to achieve your goals and priorities. Good time management skills are essential for managing workload, meeting deadlines, and maintaining work-life balance.

2. Common Time Management Challenges: Common time management challenges include:

- Overcommitment: Taking on too many tasks or responsibilities
- Procrastination: Delaying tasks or putting them off until later
- Distractions: Interruptions and distractions from other tasks or responsibilities
- Lack of focus: Difficulty focusing on one task or activity for an extended period of time

4. Approaches to Time Management: Effective time management involves using a combination of approaches and techniques, including:

- Goal setting: Setting clear and achievable goals for your tasks and responsibilities

- Prioritization: Determining the most important tasks and focusing on those first
- Task management: Breaking tasks down into smaller, more manageable parts
- Time blocking: Scheduling blocks of time for specific tasks and activities
- Delegation: Assigning tasks to others when appropriate
- Elimination of distractions: Reducing interruptions and distractions in the workplace

5. Prioritization Techniques: Effective prioritization involves determining the most important tasks and focusing on those first. There are several prioritization techniques, including:

- Urgency-Importance Matrix: This technique involves categorizing tasks into four quadrants based on their level of urgency and importance.
- Eisenhower Matrix: This technique involves categorizing tasks into four categories based on their urgency and importance.
- ABC Analysis: This technique involves categorizing tasks into three categories based on their level of importance.

6. Key Takeaways:

- Effective time management and prioritization are critical skills for any manager.
- Good time management skills can increase productivity, reduce stress, and enhance overall job satisfaction.
- Effective time management involves using a combination of approaches and techniques, including goal setting,

prioritization, task management, time blocking, delegation, and eliminating distractions.

- Effective prioritization involves determining the most important tasks and focusing on those first, using techniques such as the Urgency-Importance Matrix, Eisenhower Matrix, and ABC Analysis.

7. Implementing Time Management and Prioritization: Implementing time management and prioritization strategies in the workplace requires discipline, organization, and the ability to adapt to changes in workload and responsibilities. Here are some steps you can take to implement these strategies effectively:

- Start with a plan: Develop a plan for managing your time and prioritizing tasks, including setting goals and determining the most critical tasks.
- Track your time: Keep track of how you spend your time each day, including the amount of time spent on each task and any interruptions or distractions.
- Set aside dedicated time for essential tasks: Schedule blocks of time for important tasks and stick to the schedule as much as possible.
- Re-evaluate and adjust as needed: Regularly re-evaluate your time management and prioritization strategies and make adjustments as needed.

8. Managing Interruptions and Distractions: Interruptions and distractions are common in the workplace and can have a significant impact on time management and productivity. Here are some strategies for managing interruptions and distractions:

- Create a distraction-free environment: Identify the sources of distractions in your workspace and take steps to eliminate or minimize them.
- Use technology to manage interruptions: Use tools such as email filters and instant messaging tools to manage interruptions and distractions.
- Set boundaries: Set boundaries with coworkers and colleagues, such as avoiding meetings during certain times of the day or declining requests for help that are not essential.

9. Conclusion: Time management and prioritization are essential skills for any manager. By understanding the importance of these skills, implementing effective strategies, and managing interruptions and distractions, managers can effectively manage their time and prioritize tasks to achieve their goals and priorities. With practice and discipline, time management and prioritization can become a habit that contributes to overall success in the workplace.

Chapter 10

Setting and Achieving Goals

Setting and Achieving Goals: Goal setting is a critical component of success as a manager. By setting clear and measurable goals, managers can motivate and inspire their teams and track progress and success over time. Here are some steps for setting and achieving goals:

- Determine your priorities: Identify your top priorities and the most important goals for your team and the organization.
- Set SMART goals: Use the SMART goal-setting framework to set specific, measurable, achievable, relevant and time-bound goals.
- Communicate your goals: Share your goals with your team and communicate the importance of achieving these goals.
- Create a plan of action: Develop a plan for how you will achieve each goal, including the steps you will take, the resources you will need, and the timeline for completion.
- Track progress and make adjustments: Regularly track progress and make adjustments as needed to ensure you are on track to achieve your goals.

Leading Teams to Achieve Goals: As a manager, it is important to lead your team to achieve goals effectively. Here are some strategies for leading your team to success:

- Provide support and resources: Ensure that your team has the support and resources they need to achieve their goals, including training, tools, and resources.
- Encourage collaboration and teamwork: Foster a collaborative and supportive team environment where team members feel comfortable working together to achieve shared goals.
- Recognize and reward success: Recognize and reward team members for their contributions and successes, including milestones and accomplishments.
- Lead by example: Demonstrate your commitment to achieving goals by leading by example and setting an example for your team.

Overcoming Obstacles: Obstacles and challenges are a natural part of goal setting and achievement. Here are some strategies for overcoming obstacles and challenges:

- Anticipate obstacles: Consider potential obstacles and challenges and develop a plan for addressing them.
- Be flexible: Be open to adjusting your plan as needed to overcome obstacles and challenges.
- Seek help: Reach out to others for support and assistance when needed.
- Stay focused: Keep your goals in mind and stay focused on achieving them, even when faced with obstacles and challenges.

Continuous Improvement: It's important for managers to continually assess their performance and make improvements as needed. Here are some steps for continuous improvement:

- Reflect on your leadership style: Take time to reflect on your leadership style and how you approach goal setting and team management. Identify areas where you can improve and make changes as needed.
- Seek feedback: Ask for feedback from your team members and colleagues to gain insight into your strengths and weaknesses as a manager.
- Seek opportunities for growth and development: Seek opportunities for growth and development, such as training programs, workshops, and mentorship opportunities.
- Encourage continuous improvement in your team: Encourage your team members to continuously assess their performance and seek opportunities for growth and development.

Staying Motivated: Staying motivated is key to success as a manager. Here are some strategies for staying motivated:

- Celebrate successes: Celebrate successes, big and small, and take time to recognize the hard work and dedication of your team.
- Focus on your purpose: Stay focused on your purpose and the impact you are making on your team and organization.
- Take care of yourself: Take care of your physical, mental, and emotional health to maintain the energy and focus you need to be an effective manager.
- Stay positive: Stay positive, even in the face of challenges, and focus on opportunities for growth and improvement.

Conclusion: Becoming a better manager takes effort, commitment, and a willingness to improve continuously. By mastering the art of goal setting and team management, building trust with your team, motivating and inspiring your team, delegating responsibilities efficiently, developing your team members, managing conflict resolution, and effectively managing your time, you can become an effective and successful manager. With dedication and hard work, you can achieve your goals and drive success for your team and organization.

Chapter 11

Performance Management and Feedback

In this chapter, we will discuss the importance of performance management and feedback for the success of a team. A manager must be able to identify and address the strengths and weaknesses of their team members and create a plan to help them improve.

Section 1: The Purpose of Performance Management Performance management is an ongoing process of evaluating and improving employee performance. It involves setting goals and expectations, providing feedback, and monitoring progress. The goal of performance management is to support employee development, improve team performance, and align individual efforts with the organization's goals.

Section 2: Setting Clear Goals and Expectations One of the key elements of performance management is setting clear goals and expectations for each team member. A manager should take the time to understand each team member's strengths, weaknesses, and professional goals and use this information to set specific, measurable, and achievable targets. Goals should be reviewed and updated regularly to ensure that they remain relevant and challenging.

Section 3: Providing Constructive Feedback Providing feedback is a critical part of performance management. Feedback should be given regularly and in a timely manner. It should be constructive, focusing on specific behaviors and actions, and should provide both positive and negative feedback. Managers should also be open to receiving feedback from their team members, as this can provide valuable insights into their own leadership style and help identify areas for improvement.

Section 4: Monitoring Progress and Celebrating Success Performance management is an ongoing process, and it is important to regularly monitor progress and provide support where necessary. Celebrating successes, no matter how small, can help build team morale and motivate team members to continue working towards their goals. On the other hand, if team members are not meeting expectations, a manager should work with them to identify and address the issue and provide additional support if necessary.

Section 5: Providing Coaching and Development Opportunities A critical aspect of performance management is providing team members with opportunities to develop their skills and advance their careers. Managers should identify areas where their team members need support, provide coaching and mentorship, and help them access training and development opportunities. This not only helps to improve individual performance but also contributes to the overall success of the team.

Section 6: Handling Underperformance Despite a manager's best efforts, some team members may not meet expectations. In these cases, it is important for the manager to have a clear process for addressing underperformance. This should start with a discussion to understand the root cause of the issue and to identify any support that can be provided to help the team member improve. If the issue persists, a manager may need to take disciplinary action, which should be consistent and fair.

Section 7: Incorporating Performance Management into the Employee Evaluation Process Performance management should be incorporated into the employee evaluation process. This provides a formal opportunity for managers to provide feedback, review progress toward goals, and assess the overall performance of their team members. Employee evaluations should be a two-way conversation, with team members having the opportunity to provide feedback on their manager and the performance management process.

Performance management and feedback are powerful tools for managers to improve the performance of their teams. By setting clear goals, providing constructive feedback, monitoring progress, and providing coaching and development opportunities, a manager can help their team members reach their full potential. Handling underperformance and incorporating performance management into the employee evaluation process helps to ensure that the process is effective, fair, and supportive. By embracing performance management, a manager can build a high-performing team that is motivated, engaged, and aligned with the goals of the organization.

Chapter 12

Building a Positive Work Culture

Apositive work culture is essential for a productive, engaged, and motivated team. Positive work culture is characterized by trust, mutual respect, collaboration, and a sense of community. It fosters an environment where employees feel valued, appreciated, and empowered to do their best work. As a manager, you play a critical role in building and maintaining a positive work culture.

Creating a Sense of Community: One of the key components of a positive work culture is a sense of community. This can be achieved through a variety of ways, including:

- Encouraging team-building activities: Regular team-building activities, such as off-site retreats, lunches, and team challenges, can help build a sense of community among team members.

- Encouraging collaboration: Encouraging collaboration and teamwork can help build a sense of community and create a shared sense of purpose.

- Encouraging open communication: Encouraging open and transparent communication can help build trust and create a sense of community among team members.

1. Empowering Employees: Empowering employees is key to building a positive work culture. This can be achieved through a variety of ways, including:

- Encouraging creativity and innovation: Encouraging creativity and innovation can help employees feel valued and empowered to bring new ideas to the table.
- Providing opportunities for professional growth: Providing opportunities for professional growth, such as training and development programs, can help employees feel valued and empowered to take their careers to the next level.
- Encouraging employee voice: Encouraging employee voice through open communication and feedback mechanisms can help employees feel valued and empowered to bring their perspectives to the table.

Celebrating Success: Celebrating success is key to building a positive work culture. This can be achieved through a variety of ways, including:

- Celebrating individual and team successes: Celebrating individual and team successes, big and small, can help build a sense of pride and camaraderie among team members.
- Providing recognition and rewards: Providing recognition and rewards for exceptional performance can help employees feel valued and appreciated for their hard work.
- Creating a positive work environment: Creating a positive work environment through physical design, employee engagement activities, and other initiatives can help employees feel valued and appreciated for their contributions.

Addressing Challenges: Addressing challenges is an important part of building a positive work culture. Here are some steps for addressing challenges:

- Encouraging open communication: Encouraging open and transparent communication can help identify and address challenges before they escalate.
- Encouraging collaboration: Encouraging collaboration and teamwork can help identify and address challenges and find mutually beneficial solutions.
- Providing resources and support: Providing resources and support, such as conflict resolution training, can help employees effectively address challenges.

Building Trust: Building trust is a critical component of a positive work culture. Trust allows employees to feel safe, valued, and respected, which can lead to improved performance and job satisfaction. Here are some ways to build trust with your team:

- Lead by example: As a manager, you set the tone for the team. Lead by example by being transparent, honest, and trustworthy.
- Encourage open communication: Encourage open and transparent communication among team members. This can help build trust and create a shared sense of purpose.
- Provide clear expectations and follow through: Provide clear expectations and follow through on commitments. This can help build trust and credibility among team members.
- Foster a safe environment: Foster a safe environment by creating a culture of respect and equality. This can help build trust and create a positive work culture.

Fostering Collaboration: Fostering collaboration is a critical component of a positive work culture. Collaboration helps to build a sense of community, create a shared sense of purpose, and drive results. Here are some ways to foster collaboration with your team:

- Encourage teamwork: Encourage teamwork and collaboration by setting clear expectations, providing resources, and recognizing the value of collaboration.
- Encourage cross-functional collaboration: Encourage cross-functional collaboration by providing opportunities for team members to work together on projects and initiatives.
- Encourage diversity and inclusivity: Encourage diversity and inclusivity by creating an environment where all team members feel valued and appreciated for their contributions.

Recognizing and Celebrating Diversity: Recognizing and celebrating diversity is a critical component of a positive work culture. Diversity and inclusivity can help bring new perspectives, foster creativity, and drive innovation. Here are some ways to recognize and celebrate diversity with your team:

- Encourage diversity and inclusivity: Encourage diversity and inclusivity by creating an environment where all team members feel valued and appreciated for their contributions.
- Provide opportunities for diversity and inclusivity training: Provide opportunities for diversity and inclusivity training, such as workshops and training sessions, to help team members understand and appreciate the value of diversity.
- Celebrate diversity: Celebrate diversity by recognizing the unique contributions of all team members and recognizing the diversity of backgrounds, experiences, and perspectives.

Encouraging Employee Engagement: Encouraging employee engagement is a critical component of a positive work culture. Employee engagement can lead to improved performance, job satisfaction, and a sense of purpose. Here are some ways to encourage employee engagement:

- Encourage open communication: Encourage open and transparent communication between managers and employees. This can help build trust and create a shared sense of purpose.

- Provide opportunities for professional growth: Providing opportunities for professional growth, such as training and development programs, can help employees feel valued and empowered to take their careers to the next level.

- Foster a positive work environment: Foster a positive work environment by creating a culture of respect, equality, and appreciation. This can help build a sense of community and create a positive work culture.

Maintaining a Positive Work Culture: Maintaining a positive work culture is a continuous process. Here are some ways to maintain a positive work culture:

- Regularly assess and evaluate the work culture: Regularly assess and evaluate the work culture to identify areas for improvement and areas of strength.

- Continuously encourage and foster a positive work culture: Continuously encourage and foster a positive work culture through ongoing employee engagement activities, team-building activities, and training programs.

- Continuously celebrate success

Chapter 13

Navigating Change and Adaptability

Change is a constant in today's fast-paced business environment, and effective leaders must be able to manage and navigate it. The ability to adapt and change is essential to the success of any organization, and managers play a critical role in helping their teams to transition through changes. In this chapter, we will explore the importance of change management, the skills and strategies needed to navigate change effectively, and the impact of change on organizations and employees.

Section 1: The Importance of Change Management Change management is the process of planning and executing change in a controlled and efficient manner. Effective change management minimizes the negative impact of change on employees and the organization and maximizes the benefits of the change. It involves preparing employees for change, communicating the reasons for change, and helping employees to adjust to the new situation.

Section 2: Understanding Resistance to Change Despite the benefits of change, employees often resist it. Resistance to change can stem from fear of the unknown, a lack of trust in the change process, or a belief that the change will negatively impact their work or job security. Managers must understand these sources of resistance and be prepared to address them in order to effectively navigate change.

Section 3: Strategies for Navigating Change Managers can use a variety of strategies to navigate change and help their teams to adapt. These strategies include:

- Effective communication: Communicating the reasons for change, the benefits, and how it will impact employees can help to minimize resistance and increase acceptance.
- Involving employees in the change process: Involving employees in the planning and implementation of change can increase their sense of ownership and investment in the change.
- Providing support and resources: Providing employees with the support and resources they need to successfully navigate change can help to minimize stress and increase the chances of success.
- Building a culture of adaptability: Encouraging a culture of adaptability and continuous improvement can help to ensure that employees are better prepared to handle change.

Section 4: The Impact of Change on Employees Change can have a significant impact on employees, and managers must be prepared to support their teams through the transition. The impact of change can include stress, uncertainty, and decreased job satisfaction, but it can also lead to improved performance and increased motivation.

Section 5: The Impact of Change on Organizations In addition to its impact on employees, change can also have a significant impact on organizations. The benefits of effective change management include increased competitiveness, improved performance, and increased employee engagement and satisfaction.

Section 6: Developing a Change Management Plan Developing a change management plan is an important step in the process of navigating change. A change management plan should include the following elements:

- Defining the change: What is the change, and what are its goals and objectives?
- Identifying stakeholders: Who will be impacted by the change, and what are their interests and needs?
- Assessing the impact of change: What is the expected impact of the change on employees, the organization, and other stakeholders?
- Developing a communication plan: How will the change be communicated to employees and other stakeholders, and what messages need to be communicated?
- Identifying potential risks and challenges: What are the potential risks and challenges associated with the change, and how will they be addressed?
- Providing support and resources: What support and resources will be provided to employees and other stakeholders to help them navigate the change?
- Evaluating the success of the change: How will the success of the change be evaluated, and what metrics will be used?

Section 7: Managing the Implementation of Change Once the change management plan has been developed, the next step is to manage the implementation of the change. This involves the following steps:

- Communicating the change: Communicating the change to employees and other stakeholders in a clear and concise manner.

- Providing training and support: Providing employees with the training and support they need to successfully navigate the change.

- Monitoring progress: Monitoring progress and tracking progress against the change management plan.

- Making adjustments as needed: Making adjustments to the change management plan as needed to ensure its success.

- Evaluating the success of the change: Evaluating the success of the change and making improvements for future changes.

Section 8: Continuously Improving the Change Process Continuously improving the change process is an important aspect of effective change management. This involves regularly reviewing the change process, identifying areas for improvement, and making changes to ensure that future changes are managed more effectively.

Navigating change and adaptability are essential skills for managers in today's fast-paced business environment. Effective change management can help to minimize the negative impact of change and maximize its benefits. By developing a change management plan, managing the implementation of change, and continuously improving the change process, managers can help their teams to successfully navigate change and achieve their goals.

Chapter 14

Managing Remote Teams

The rise of remote work has changed the way managers lead and manage their teams. Remote teams bring their own set of unique challenges, including communication barriers, lack of face-to-face interaction, and difficulties in establishing and maintaining trust. However, with the right approach, managers can effectively manage remote teams and drive business results.

Section 1: Building Strong Communication with Remote Teams Strong communication is the key to managing remote teams successfully. Managers need to establish clear and consistent communication channels, set expectations for communication, and encourage open and honest communication. This includes regular virtual team meetings, regular check-ins, and clear guidelines for communication and collaboration.

Section 2: Fostering a Sense of Community Fostering a sense of community is important for remote teams as it helps to build trust and enhance collaboration. Managers can foster a sense of community by regularly scheduling virtual team-building activities, encouraging team members to share their personal lives, and promoting collaboration and teamwork.

Section 3: Providing Clear Expectations and Guidelines Providing clear expectations and guidelines is important for remote teams, as it helps to minimize confusion and misunderstandings. This includes setting clear work hours, expectations for response times, and guidelines for collaboration and teamwork.

Section 4: Managing Performance and Productivity Managing performance and productivity can be more challenging with remote teams, as managers cannot observe their team members' work in person. Managers can manage performance and productivity by setting clear goals and expectations, regularly monitoring progress, and providing regular feedback and support.

Section 5: Addressing Challenges Remote work can bring its own set of challenges, such as feelings of isolation, lack of motivation, and difficulty with collaboration. Managers need to be proactive in addressing these challenges and finding solutions to ensure their remote teams remain engaged and productive.

Section 6: Leveraging Technology Technology plays a critical role in managing remote teams, and managers need to be familiar with and leverage the right tools to support communication, collaboration, and productivity. This includes video conferencing tools, project management tools, and virtual collaboration platforms. Managers should ensure that their remote teams have access to the right technology and that it is being used effectively.

Section 7: Encouraging Work-Life Balance Encouraging work-life balance is important for remote teams, as remote workers often struggle with separating their work and personal lives. Managers should set clear boundaries for work hours, encourage regular breaks, and promote a healthy work-life balance.

Section 8: Managing Remote Team Members Individually Every team member is unique, and managing remote team members effectively requires a personalized approach. Managers should get to know their team members, understand their strengths and weaknesses, and provide individualized support and feedback. This will help to foster a positive and productive work environment and enhance overall performance.

Section 9: Celebrating Success and Recognizing Contributions Celebrating success and recognizing contributions is important for remote teams, as it helps to boost morale and foster a sense of belonging. Managers should regularly celebrate team and individual successes and recognize the contributions of team members. This can be done through virtual celebrations, bonuses, or recognition programs.

Section 10: Continuously Improving Managing remote teams is an ongoing process and requires continuous improvement. Managers should regularly evaluate their approach, gather feedback from their team members, and make adjustments as needed to ensure that they are effectively managing their remote teams.

Managing remote teams requires a different approach than managing traditional in-person teams, but with the right skills, tools, and mindset, managers can effectively lead and manage their remote teams to success. By leveraging technology, encouraging work-life balance, managing team members individually, celebrating success and recognizing contributions, and continuously improving, managers can create a positive and productive work environment for their remote teams.

Chapter 15

Staying Current with Industry Trends and Best Practices

In today's rapidly changing business landscape, it's critical for managers to stay informed about the latest trends and best practices in their industry. Staying current with industry trends and best practices can help managers stay ahead of the competition, make informed decisions, and continuously improve their leadership skills.

Section 1: Staying Informed Staying informed about industry trends and best practices requires continuous learning and engagement. Managers can attend industry conferences, read trade publications, and network with other professionals to stay informed about the latest trends and best practices.

Section 2: Developing a Learning Plan Developing a learning plan is a critical component of staying current with industry trends and best practices. Managers should set aside time each week or month for learning and professional development. This may include reading books, attending webinars, or participating in online courses.

Section 3: Networking Networking is an important component of staying informed about industry trends and best practices. Managers should attend industry events, join professional organizations, and connect with other professionals in their field to learn about the latest trends and best practices.

Section 4: Implementing Best Practices Implementing best practices is the key to staying ahead of the competition. Managers should carefully review the best practices in their industry and determine which ones are most relevant to their organization. They should then work with their teams to implement these best practices and continuously evaluate their effectiveness.

Section 5: Staying Adaptable Staying adaptable and open to change is critical in today's fast-paced business environment. Managers should be willing to embrace new trends and best practices and continuously evaluate and update their approaches to ensure that they are staying current with the latest industry trends and best practices.

Section 6: Continuously Evaluate and Improve Continuous evaluation and improvement are key to staying current with industry trends and best practices. Managers should regularly assess the effectiveness of their approach to staying informed, implementing best practices, and adapting to change. They should identify areas for improvement and make changes as necessary to stay ahead of the competition and continuously improve their leadership skills.

Section 7: Encouraging Team Members to Stay Current Encouraging team members to stay informed about industry trends and best practices is a critical component of building a competitive and successful organization. Managers should encourage their team members to attend industry events, read trade publications, and participate in professional development opportunities to stay current with the latest trends and best practices.

Section 8: Keeping Up with Technological Trends Technology is rapidly changing and has a major impact on many industries. Managers must stay informed about the latest technological trends and best practices to stay ahead of the competition and ensure that their organization is well-positioned to take advantage of new opportunities.

Section 9: Staying Ahead of the Competition Staying current with industry trends and best practices can help managers stay ahead of the competition. By staying informed, implementing best practices, and continuously evaluating and improving their approach, managers can ensure that their organization is well-positioned to compete in today's rapidly changing business landscape.

Conclusion: Staying current with industry trends and best practices is critical for managers who want to lead their organizations to success. By staying informed, developing a learning plan, networking, implementing best practices, and continuously evaluating and improving, managers can stay ahead of the competition and continuously improve their leadership skills. By encouraging their team members to stay current, managers can build a competitive and successful organization that is well-positioned to thrive in today's rapidly changing business landscape.

414 Industries Online Courses

We never stop learning. Check out other books by Jules Beshears and 414 Industries

https://414industries.com/

https://www.instagram.com/414industries/

https://www.facebook.com/414industries